Tow Trucks
Grúas

Joanne Randolph

...ucción al español:
Eduardo Alamán

PowerKiDS & **Editorial Buenas Letras**™
press. New York

For Riley, Deming, and Hannah

Published in 2008 by The Rosen Publishing Group, Inc.
29 East 21st Street, New York, NY 10010

First Edition

Book Design: Greg Tucker
Photo Researcher: Nicole Pristash

Photo Credits: Cover, pp. 9, 11, 13, 15, 24 (bottom) Shutterstock.com; p. 5 © Matt Matthews/iStockphoto.com; p. 7 © Terry Wilson/iStockphoto.com; p. 17 © Logan Mock-Bunting/Getty Images; p. 19 © Doug Pensinger/Getty Images; p. 21 © Jack Guez/AFP/Getty Images; p. 23 © Branko Miokovic/iStockphoto.com.

Cataloging Data

Randolph, Joanne.
   Tow Trucks–Gruas / Joanne Randolph; traducción al español: Eduardo Alamán.— 1st ed.
      p. cm. — (To the rescue!–¡Al rescate!).
   Includes index.
   ISBN 978-1-4042-7675-8 (library binding)
   1. Wreckers (Vehicles)—Juvenile literature. 2. Automobiles—Towing—Juvenile literature.
3. Spanish language materials I. Title.

Manufactured in the United States of America

Websites: Due to the changing nature of Internet links, PowerKids Press and Editorial Buenas Letras have developed an online list of Web sites related to the subject of this book. This site is updated regularly. Please use this link to access the list: www.powerkidslinks.com/ttr/ttruck/

Contents/Contenido

Anytime there is trouble on the road, tow trucks are there. Tow trucks are important helpers.

Cuando hay problemas en el camino, las grúas están ahí para ayudarnos. Las grúas ofrecen una importante ayuda.

Tow trucks move cars off the road. Moving the cars quickly keeps other drivers safe.

Las grúas sacan del camino a los autos que tienen problemas. Sacar a estos autos mantiene los caminos seguros.

Tow trucks pull cars and trucks when they cannot move.

Cuando los autos o camiones no pueden moverse, las grúas los sacan del problema.

Some tow trucks have **flatbeds** in the back to carry broken-down cars or trucks.

Algunas grúas tienen una **plataforma** para llevar autos o camiones descompuestos.

Some tow trucks have a special arm on the back that pulls a car or truck behind them.

Algunas grúas tienen un brazo especial para remolcar a los autos o camiones.

13

Some tow trucks are built to pull airplanes into place. This takes a very strong tow truck!

Algunas grúas se construyen para remolcar aviones. ¡Para este trabajo se necesita una grúa muy fuerte!

Tow trucks can help a driver who is trapped in his or her car by a **flood**.

Las grúas pueden ayudar a personas atrapadas en su auto durante una **inundación**.

Sometimes tow trucks do special jobs. This tow truck moves cars out of the way at a **racetrack**.

A veces, las grúas hacen tareas especiales. Esta grúa remolca autos de una **pista de carreras**.

Tow trucks can even move large buses and other trucks.

Las grúas pueden mover grandes autobuses y otros camiones.

Tow trucks play a big part in keeping our roads safe.

Las grúas tienen una función importante. ¡Las grúas mantienen nuestros caminos seguros!

flatbed / (la) plataforma

flood / (la) inundación

racetrack / (la) pista de carreras

Index   Índice